CARCICH at 7:30

CARCICH at 7:30

Sermons Preached at Camp Meetings By Theodore Carcich

Southern Publishing Association, Nashville, Tennessee

Library of Congress
Catalog Card Number: 74-30869
SBN 8127-0091-0

This book was
Edited by Don Short
Designed by Dean Tucker
Cover portrait by Buford Winfrey

Type set 11/13 Optima
Printed on No. 66 Antique
Cover stock: Carolina C1S

Printed in U.S.A.

Dedicated

To the vast army of gospel workers proclaiming the everlasting gospel throughout the world.

Contents

Biblical Versions

In addition to the King James Version of the Bible and the Revised Standard Version, the following versions have been quoted:

(Phillips), The New Testament in Modern English. Copyright, J. B. Phillips, 1958. Used by permission of The Macmillan Company.

(NEB), The New English Bible. Copyright, The Delegates of the Oxford University Press and The Syndics of the Cambridge University Press, 1961, 1970. Reprinted by permission.

(TEV), Today's English Version of the New Testament. Copyright, American Bible Society, 1966, 1971.

(TLB), Taylor. The Living Bible, Paraphrased (Wheaton: Tyndale House, 1971). Used by permission.

What Next?

We live under the prospect of imminent destruction. The explosion of the hydrogen bomb at Eniwetok Atoll impressed this fear upon our minds. The bomb was a thousand times more powerful than the one that fell on Hiroshima, or the equivalent of between two million and five million tons of TNT. The blast practically obliterated the atoll, sending a flame two miles wide and five miles up in the air.

An explosion of this size would totally devastate an area of one hundred fifty square miles. In addition, a searing heat would radiate over an area of eight hundred square miles. The bomb would certainly start a fire storm such as raged in Hamburg and Hiroshima. Fire storms fan their own flames by creating their own draft.

Finally, the explosion of the bomb would contribute, in a small yet measurable way, noxious gas to the earth's already polluted atmosphere. It could well lead to the extinction of life on the planet.

Is it any wonder that men everywhere anxiously

ask, "What next?" All are convinced that some great cataclysmic event faces the world, but many don't know what event. What does Bible prophecy predict? Will man wipe himself out by his own invention? Will a group of nations force their will by military might upon the rest of the world? Or will God end the chaos and inaugurate an eternal era of peace and happiness?

The Certainty of the Second Coming of Christ

Having tried every form of government in an endeavor to secure peace and harmony between nations, man finds himself at the end of the trail. Faced by the perils of his own inventions and the godless philosophies that would destroy spiritual and moral values, man stands in desperate need of having someone greater than himself intervene in human affairs. And this God proposes to do by the personal, imminent, and glorious return of Jesus Christ to this earth. The doctrine of Christ's second coming is the very keynote of Sacred Scripture.

The gospel of Jesus Christ is incomplete without the doctrine of His second coming. The importance of the second coming of Christ parallels the importance of His first coming. As surely as the Incarnation led to the cross, and the cross to the grave, and the empty grave to the ascension, so the ascension leads to His coming again in glory.

The certainty of Christ's second coming does not

rest upon some church dogma but upon the authoritative statements of Christ, the angels, and the apostles. Christ promised, "I will come again"; "the Son of man shall come" (John 14:3; Matthew 16:27).

With certainty the angels at Christ's ascension said, "This same Jesus, which is taken up from you into heaven, shall so come in like manner as ye have seen him go into heaven" (Acts 1:11).

The apostles swell the chorus of certainty. Paul stated that "the Lord himself shall return from heaven," and "Christ . . . shall . . . appear the second time" (1 Thessalonians 4:16; Hebrews 9:28). Peter adds, "The chief Shepherd shall appear" (1 Peter 5:4). John testifies, "He cometh with clouds; and every eye shall see him" (Revelation 1:7).

The Certainty That His Coming Is Near

While no man knows the exact day or hour of Christ's return, all men may know when His coming is near. Christ gave this information when He answered the questions "Tell us, when shall these things be? and what shall be the sign of thy coming, and of the end of the world?" (Matthew 24:3). The disciples raised the question because Christ had previously talked to them about the destruction of Jerusalem and the end of the world.

In answer to the first, Christ said, "And when ye shall see Jerusalem compassed with armies, then know that the desolation thereof is nigh" (Luke 21: 20). In AD 66 when Cestius the Roman came against Jerusalem, he unaccountably withdrew, and the Christians discerned in this the sign foretold by Christ and fled. The following year the Romans resumed the siege and, according to Josephus, over one million Jews perished by the time the city capitulated in AD 70. During the frightful days of the siege, mothers ate their own children in direct fulfillment of Moses' prophecy in Deuteronomy 28:47-53. The Romans destroyed the city and completely demolished the temple.

Notice the prophetic words of Christ as to what would immediately follow the destruction of Jerusalem and the dispersion of the Jews. "*For then shall be great tribulation,* such as was not since the beginning of the world to this time, no, nor ever shall be" (Matthew 24:21).

History confirms the persecution of the Christians in the first three centuries under the pagan Roman emperors and also the greater and more terrible persecution during the long centuries of papal supremacy.

The Signs of His Coming Follow the Tribulation

Next in the divine schedule come the signs preceding Christ's coming. Concerning these signs, the Master, after describing the destruction of Jerusalem and the tribulation that would follow, said, "*Immediately after* the tribulation of those days shall the sun be darkened, and the moon shall not give her light, and the stars shall fall from heaven" (Matthew 24:29). The following facts can be ascertained in any public library:

1. Sun and moon darkened, May 19, 1780.

2. Greatest display of falling stars, November 13, 1833. The celestial displays came in harmony with the divine timetable.

There are additional signs—not in the heavens, but upon the earth. Notice the sequence of events: "And upon the earth distress of nations, with perplexity; the sea and the waves roaring; men's hearts failing them for fear, and for looking after those things which are coming on the earth" (Luke 21:25, 26). Daily our newspapers and radios literally shout at us that the divine sequence is meeting fulfillment.

1. "Distress of nations"—the present chaotic world condition.

2. "Sea and waves roaring"—destructive storms on land and sea.

3. "Men's hearts failing them"—men everywhere giving up hope.

In the midst of these unmistakable signs men will witness a still greater sign. Said Christ, "And this gospel of the kingdom shall be preached in all the world for a witness unto all nations; and then shall the end come" (Matthew 24:14). Never before have we seen such an interest in Bible study and especially in Bible prophecy. The Bible, still the best seller, is being sold and distributed by the millions. Religionists are restudying the theme of Christ's return. Men everywhere expect some world-shaking event to take place, and many rightly believe it is the long-heralded and the long-awaited return of Jesus Christ to this earth.

What Next?

"What next?" cry the politician, the scientist, the businessman. Who is qualified to answer this question? Only He who has accurately outlined the divine schedule for human history—the Lord Jesus Christ Himself.

In plain and simple language that all can understand, Christ tells us that the next great event is His return to the earth in glory—not some time in the far distant future, but in the close proximity and sequence as our Lord has outlined. "And *then* shall appear the sign of the Son of man in heaven: and then shall all the tribes of the earth mourn, and they shall see the Son of man coming in the clouds of heaven with power and great glory" (Matthew 24:30). The divine schedule is certain, the final event sure.

Are You Ready for That Event?

When that day arrives, there will be a great prayer meeting, the largest ever held on this earth. People may feel reluctant about attending prayer meeting, but here is one they will attend. But that day will find many not ready. Because of their unprepared condition, "then shall all the tribes of the earth mourn" (Matthew 24:30).

It will be a sad gathering, for it will be held too late. Too late will men realize that they have offered their last prayer, preached their last sermon, made their last appeal. Together rich and poor, learned and ignorant, famous and obscure, will mingle their tears as they sigh in bitter regret over having failed to make preparation to meet their Lord in peace. Often they had heard this warning: "Be ye also ready: for in such an hour as ye think not the Son of man cometh" (Matthew 24:44). They heard, but heeded it not. Now with bitter lament they cry out in anguish of soul, "The harvest is past, the summer is ended, and we are not saved" (Jeremiah 8:20).

The last great day is near. Property and fame will be worthless. Money will not buy anything. Mansions and hovels, jewel-decked garments and rags, will perish together. On that day worldly pleasure will suddenly and tragically end.

You Can Be Ready!

Which class are you in today? There will be only two classes when the Lord returns—those who are ready and those who are not. It was so in Noah's day. It will be so when the Lord returns. The Bible clearly teaches that some will be found ready. When the Lord returns they will exclaim, "Lo, this is our God; we have waited for him, and he will save us" (Isaiah 25:9). To such, Christ will reply, "Come, ye blessed of my Father, inherit the kingdom prepared for you from the foundation of the world" (Matthew 25:34).

How can you get ready? Listen to Christ's answer: "Not every one that saith unto me, Lord, Lord, shall enter into the kingdom of heaven; but he that doeth the will of my Father which is in heaven" (Matthew 7:21). You need not be lost. You can be among the redeemed.

A Look Into the Future

No man can unlock the door of the future. Even the wisest man cannot penetrate the secrets of futurity. Anyone, however, can make a shrewd guess. When Croesus consulted the Delphian oracle as to his contemplated war against the Persians, he was told he would destroy a great empire. That was a safe prediction, for whether Croesus or the Persians were victorious in the war, a great empire would be destroyed.

Seneca the Roman predicted that one day the Shetland Islands would no longer mark the limits of the inhabited world. That also was a sensible prediction, but it was not prophecy. An astronomer can foretell heavenly movements a long time in advance. He can predict solar eclipses to the minute. This, however, is calculation, not prophecy.

What, then, is prophecy? Prophecy is to name a certain city or nation, spell out its probationary time, and then name the kingdom or conqueror who will destroy it. This is prophecy, the sort of thing we meet in the Old and New Testaments.

Claiming to be a prophet, Jeane Dixon, of Washington, D.C., also admits some miscalculations. Not so with Daniel, the prophet of God, for the accuracy of his predictions is substantiated by history. As an example, consider the seventh chapter of his book where God outlines world history from the days of Babylon until the end of time. Anyone concerned about the future should heed this startling prophecy.

"Daniel spake and said, I saw in my vision by night, and, behold, the four winds of the heaven strove upon the great sea. And four great beasts came up from the sea, diverse one from another" (Daniel 7:2, 3).

The prophecy depicts political strife and war among nations resulting in the rise and fall of four great world kingdoms or empires. We shall take the four beasts or kingdoms in the order presented and permit history to document the certainty of the prophecy.

Babylon

Prophecy: "The first was like a lion, and had eagle's wings: I beheld till the wings thereof were plucked, and it was lifted up from the earth, and made stand upon the feet as a man, and a man's heart was given to it" (Daniel 7:4).

History: The lion fittingly represents Babylon, the first great world kingdom. "The only large object that has ever appeared within the ruins of Babylon," says Rassam, "was the monolith of a lion." The eagle's wings are suggestive of the power and swiftness of Babylonian armies. The "man's heart . . . given to it" indicates that the lionlike prowess would be replaced by weakness and timidity. The early rulers of the Neo-Babylonian Empire, Nabopolassar and Nebuchadnezzar, possessed the courage and strength of a lion. At the time of the overthrow of Babylon by the Medes and Persians the profligate and weak-kneed Belshazzar occupied the throne.

Medo-Persia

Prophecy: "And behold another beast, a second, like to a bear, and it raised up itself on one side, and it had three ribs in the mouth of it between the teeth of it: and they said thus unto it, Arise, devour much flesh" (Daniel 7:5).

History: The verse accurately pictures the dual empire of Medo-Persia, the successor to Babylon. At first the Medes dominated, then the Persians gained the ascendancy, fulfilling the prophetic description of the bear that "raised up itself on one side." The statement "devour much flesh" symbolizes the Persians' vast conquests, ranging from the Indus River to the Aegean Sea, including Lydia, Egypt, and Babylon, aptly portrayed by the "three ribs in the mouth of it." The empire collapsed when the Greeks under Alexander killed Darius Codomannus at the battle of Arbela in 331 BC.

Greece

Prophecy: "After this I beheld, and lo another, like a leopard, which had upon the back of it four wings of a fowl; the beast had also four heads; and dominion was given to it" (Daniel 7:6).

History: The leopardlike beast with four wings characterizes the swift and bounding military conquests of the Greeks under Alexander the Great. In three years' time he swept from Macedonia to the River Ganges in India. The prophecy foretold the fourfold division of his vast kingdom in the phrase "the beast had also four heads." Alexander died in 323 BC, and his four generals divided the empire. Cassander ruled Macedonia and Greece, Ptolemy ruled Egypt, Lysimachus ruled Thrace and Asia Minor, and Seleucus ruled Syria and Babylonia. Grecian supremacy ended when the Romans shattered the Greek forces at Pydna in 168 BC.

Rome

Prophecy: "After this I saw in the night visions, and behold a fourth beast, dreadful and terrible, and strong exceedingly; and it had great iron teeth: it devoured and brake in pieces, and stamped the residue with the feet of it: and it was diverse from all the beasts that were before it; and it had ten horns" (Daniel 7:7).

History: Here the prophet portrays Rome, the same

empire represented by the iron of Nebuchadnezzar's image in Daniel 2. Nothing could stop Rome as it swept over all opposition in achieving world conquest. In the words of the prophecy: It "brake in pieces, and stamped the residue with the feet of it."

The prophecy foretold the breakup of Rome in the ten horns which the prophecy described as "the ten kings that shall arise" (Daniel 7:24). In fulfillment, history narrates the onslaught of the barbarian tribes of northern Europe as they overran Rome between AD 351 and 476, establishing themselves as the nations occupying the territory of the shattered empire.

Historians frequently enumerate the ten divisions of Rome as the Alamanni in Germany, the Franks in France, the Burgundians in Switzerland and southeast France, the Suevi in Portugal, the Anglo-Saxons in England, the Visigoths in Spain, the Lombards in northern Italy, the Heruli in Italy, the Vandals in North Africa, and the Ostrogoths around the head of the Adriatic.

The "little horn" that "shall arise after them" and before whom three would fall has all the earmarks of a religiopolitical power. Did any such power arise among the ten divisions of Rome?

Rise of a Religious Power

Prophecy: "And another shall rise after them; and he shall be diverse from the first, and he shall subdue three kings. And he shall speak great words against the most High, and shall wear out the saints of the most High, and think to change times and laws: and they shall be given into his hand until a time and times and the dividing of time" (Daniel 7:24, 25).

Notice these identifying factors:

1. It would arise "after" the ten kings (verse 24).

2. It would pluck up three kingdoms to make room for itself (verse 8).

3. It would be "more stout" and "diverse" from the others (verses 20 and 24).

4. It would "speak great words against the most High" (verse 25).

5. It would persecute dissenters (verse 25).

6. It would "think to change times and laws" (verse 25).

History: Early in the fourth century Constantine gave state recognition to the Christian church. At this same time Arius introduced his heretical views on the origin and nature of Christ. While the Council of Nicaea condemned Arianism, certain kingdoms accepted the heresy. Conflict developed between these powers (Heruli, Vandals, and Ostrogoths) and the rest of Christendom in the west. By the early part of the sixth century, the armies of Emperor Justinian from Constantinople wiped out—"plucked up by the roots"—these three kingdoms.

With no emperor of strength on the throne in Rome and all religious opposition removed, the Roman pontiff or bishop now stepped up to the vacant throne of the Caesars. In reality, he became "more stout" than the other kingdoms.

A candid reading of history brings to light the persecution of the Waldenses, the Lollards, the Bohemians, and the Albigenses. The Inquisition in Spain and Italy, the ferocity of the Duke of Alva in the Netherlands, the Massacre of St. Bartholomew's Day, and the oppression of the Huguenots are known to all. The prophecy states that this power would "wear out the saints of the most High."

It would also "think to change times and laws." Let one compare the second, fourth, and tenth commandments of the Decalogue in any Bible with the same in a Roman Catholic catechism and notice the difference. Despite these changes, God's commandments remain the same. They have never been altered in any way by God.

The prophecy states that the little horn's supremacy would last for a "time and times and the dividing of time" (verse 25). In Revelation the same time period is referred to as "a time, and times, and half a time" (Revelation 12:14), "a thousand two hundred and threescore days" (verse 6), and "forty and two months" (Revelation 11:2). In prophecy a day represents a year, and so the prophet here describes the 1260-year period of papal supremacy from AD 538 to 1798.

From 1798 on the shackles of religious and political despotism were stricken from men's minds by the revolutionary forces of the age. With the renaissance of learning and inventive science came a revival of nationalism and strife for supremacy. Ideologies and philosophies hitherto unknown arose and contended for the minds of men, each one claiming to be the sole arbiter of man's destiny. All are antagonistic toward each other. Catholicism, Protestantism, Islam, and political atheism will brook no rivals. Which will dominate the world? Who will take over the empire?

Let God's unerring prophecy supply the answer: "But the judgment shall sit, and they shall take away his [the little horn's] dominion, to consume and to destroy it unto the end. And the kingdom and dominion, and the greatness of the kingdom under the whole heaven, shall be given to the people of the saints of the most High, whose kingdom is an everlasting kingdom, and all dominions shall serve and obey him" (Daniel 7:26, 27).

This means that the next great and lasting event of human history is not the permanent revival of any religious power, or the universal acceptance of any political ideology, but the personal and glorious return of Jesus Christ as Lord of lords and King of kings, for "all dominions shall serve and obey him." At that time the prayer now uttered by millions, "thy kingdom come," will be realized.

Why Scoffers?

Scoffers are not a new breed. From time immemorial cynics have exulted in derision, ridicule, and biting jest.

Consider Noah's day. Men lampooned Noah unmercifully for building the ark. They called him naïve, but they drowned.

At a later date, calloused libertines regarded Lot as a simple-minded clod for believing that fire would destroy Sodom and Gomorrah. Even Lot's sons-in-law joined in the sneering banter, but they and their dissolute friends perished in the raging inferno.

Was it any different in Christ's day? You would expect so, but the taunts and jibes continued. "God, a babe born in a barn? without a father on earth or a mother in heaven?" "God, a man, living, dying, resurrected, and ascended? Incredible! Scientifically impossible! Who could believe such a thing?"

Well, a few simple shepherds, not knowing much, believed. From the east came a few Wise Men who, knowing much, also believed. In addition, twelve ordinary men and an intellectual called Paul believed, and their testimony profoundly affected history. Without question, the shepherds, the Wise Men, the apostles, by faith perceived what science could not see. As for the scoffers—they perished in the destruction of Jerusalem in AD 70.

We would wish a different fate for our generation. Regretfully, this seems not to be. We can only stop and wonder at a generation rushing headlong toward the same precipice of scorn and unbelief from which former generations plunged into oblivion.

Our enlightened age, rather than profiting from the past, utilizes intelligence to give irreligious scoffing an entirely new dimension and approach. Pious terminology notwithstanding, any derision which devaluates God and morals is irreligious.

In years past, attacks upon Biblical faith and belief originated with those outside the church. Today the blows come from within the church. Men clothed in clerical garb, charged with important functions in Christendom, and obsessed with adapting Christianity to the modern mind, project astonishing and dangerous concepts of God, Christ, and the Holy Spirit.

Every fundamental fact of Inspiration—divinity, incarnation, atonement, resurrection, the second coming of Christ—is being questioned by theological innovators and revised to square with the thinking of those who wish to profess Christianity but not be bound by its discipline. Adorned with theological jargon and presented with a flair of profound intelligence and research, these human opinions effectively serve to devaluate God in the minds of men.

As an example: By juggling Scripture and making it speak in the sense desired, the theological revilers contend that Jesus of Nazareth, although singular in character and personality, was merely a village prophet who made a deep impression upon His disciples. After His death, the theory continues, the disciples convinced themselves that those who met Jesus had been confronted by God, secretly, within the heart. This, the scoffers assure us, is substantially all there is to know.

The cynics would have us believe that the early Christians imagined vivid narratives in picture-language to symbolize this "existential experience," and that those tales now make up the Gospels and Epistles of the New Testament. In particular, they argue, the disciples could not bring themselves to believe that Jesus died; therefore, by an overwrought imagination, they made up the Resurrection story to set forth this conviction.

Let it be understood that the modern cynics cannot claim any distinction in trying to explain away the resurrection of Jesus Christ from the dead. Centuries ago the unbelievers of Christ's day tried to rationalize the resurrection of our Lord in the following manner:

"Now when they were going, behold, some of the watch [soldiers] came into the city, and shewed unto the chief priests all the things that were done. And when they were assembled with the elders, and had taken counsel, they gave large money unto the soldiers, saying, Say ye, His disciples came by night, and stole him away while we slept. And if this come to the governor's ears, we will persuade him, and secure you. So they took the money, and did as they were taught: and this saying is commonly reported among the Jews until this day" (Matthew 28:11-15).

The ancient scoffers sound as silly as their modern counterparts. Can you imagine the apostles walking over the sleeping Roman soldiers, one by one, cracking twigs and making other noises, then rolling back the stone and picking up the body of Jesus, going back out again on those cracking twigs, and getting away with the whole thing?

Today theologians in high church circles dismiss the Biblical portrait of Christ as a product of man's imagination. The devaluation of God's Word lowers Christian morals. It could not be otherwise. Why be concerned about absolute precepts and commandments from above if God does not exist? Accordingly, claim the apostles of doubt, the Ten Commandments are out of date and modern man needs a new moral ethic which makes any conceivable act morally acceptable in the "right" situation.

The new ethic, or morality, rests on the denial of any permanently binding moral laws. What may have been right or wrong centuries ago is not necessarily so today, suggests Bishop J. A. Robinson. In his book *Christian Morals Today* the bishop states, "There are no unbreakable rules" and consequently no "lists of things which are 'sins' *per se*."

An outgrowth of the new ethic is society's growing moral jungle infested by men whose only concept of a right situation is selfish interest. Shorn of Christian morality, guided by an ethic whose definition is a pure abstraction, modern man now decides for himself what is right regarding his neighbor's house, wife, and goods. No police force can capably cope with this type of lawless mentality. Is it any wonder that the national crime rate is skyrocketing?

Removing God and His commandments from the thinking of men effectively obviates concern for a judgment and the return of Jesus Christ. Jeering at the second coming of Christ comes naturally to those who scorn moral restraints and make self-indulgence the norm of existence. Why anticipate an event that terminates lustful and sensual living? We never had it so good, brags the scoffer.

As the generations of the past did, so the present generation of men will continue in lawlessness until it is everlastingly too late.

Warned the apostle Peter, "There shall come in the last days scoffers, . . . saying, Where is the promise of his coming?" "But the day of the Lord will come as a thief in the night; in the which the heavens shall pass away with a great noise, and the elements shall melt with fervent heat, the earth also and the works that are therein shall be burned up" (2 Peter 3:3, 4, 10).

When man rejects the authority of God, Christ, and the Ten Commandments, the authority of human lust takes over. The growing immorality and perversity is the death rattle of an age that has rejected God and His authority.

All of us would do well to heed the apostle who said, "Seeing then that all these things shall be dissolved, what manner of persons ought ye to be in all holy conversation and godliness, looking for and hasting unto the coming of the day of God, wherein the heavens being on fire shall be dissolved, and the elements shall melt with fervent heat? Nevertheless we, according to his promise, look for new heavens and a new earth, wherein dwelleth righteousness" (2 Peter 3:11-13).

Why listen to scoffers? They guessed wrong in Noah's, Lot's, and Christ's day. They are guessing wrong today.

Let scoffers scoff. Christ lives and Christ will return. Believe Him.

After Christmas—What?

Christmas supposedly commemorates the first advent of Christ. Financially and economically this season involves more people than any other of the year. Consider the tremendous amount of buying, selling, card writing, and traveling—all because of Christmas.

Among other things, Americans spend approximately $200 million for dazzling wrapping paper, ribbons, and bows to dress up the estimated one billion gifts exchanged on December 25. Amid cries of "Oh, it's so pretty! I hate to open it!" the packages are torn open and the glittering wrappings discarded and forgotten.

Pretty packages have their place. However, with the greater portion of the world's population hungry, poorly clad, and sick, it seems that spending millions for something that goes up in smoke the day after Christmas is alien to the spirit of Christ. He showed His concern for the unfortunate when He said: "I assure you that whatever you did for the humblest of my brothers you did for me" (Matthew 25:40, Phillips).

Just suppose that Christians involved themselves as seriously in preparing for the Second Advent as they do in the celebration of the First. Think of the startling changes that would take place in the lives of people. To be specific, pride, envy, prejudice, and the seeking for preeminence would disappear. If men everywhere made it their business in life to get ready for the return of our Lord, the revolutionary effects at home and in churches would equal Pentecost.

The celebration of Christ's first advent has no point or purpose apart from a preparation for the second coming. Christ's first coming was only the beginning. He arose from the grave and ascended into heaven to complete that which He began at Bethlehem, and when His priestly mediation is finished He will return to earth in power and glory. Anyone who disbelieves the Second Advent has no reason to celebrate the First.

Why do men celebrate the one and shun preparing for the other? Basically because they do not know Christ and dread facing Him. Most people celebrate Christmas without ever seeing Christ in it. It provides a day for exchanging gifts, a big meal, and an afternoon football game on television. It is entirely possible for one to get into a seasonal mood by singing carols, participating in the festivities, and even going to church, yet never coming face-to-face with Christ as a personal Saviour.

Not so with the Second Advent. This event does not confront people with a festival but with a Person who comes to judge the living and the dead. Whether they wish it or not, all humanity will participate in this awesome event—some to their eternal gain, others to their eternal loss.

Which it will be—and it will be one or the other—depends upon that which the individual anticipates most. Those who look and prepare for the Second Advent will manifest the same intensity and desire that the shepherds and Wise Men exhibited in looking for the Infant at His coming the first time. While almost anyone can celebrate Christmas, only those who are prepared will joyfully welcome Christ at His return to earth. At that time those looking for Him will exclaim, "Lo, this is our God; we have waited for him, and he will save us: this is the Lord; we have waited for him, we will be glad and rejoice in his salvation" (Isaiah 25:9).

Sad to say, the apparent religious fervor associated with Christmas dies abruptly on December 26. People revert suddenly to their old ways and start snarling at each other just as they did prior to the Christmas season. They resume (if they ever quit) gambling, cheating at school exams, shoplifting, drunken driving, and other evils with a recklessness that belies any recent association with the hallowed story of Bethlehem. All this causes one to wonder whether the celebrants' concern centers in Christ's birth or in personal gain.

One thing is sure: the season, as now celebrated, does little to enhance the spiritual and moral life of the nation. Crime continues to rise and church attendance to dip in spite of the religious emotion whipped up annually from November 15 to December 25 in the name of Christ.

Christians should take a new look at this season of the year and also look beyond Christmas to the second advent of our Lord. Failure to look beyond leaves nothing except the tinsel and decorations which burn on the rubbish heap the day after Christmas.

Does Love Annul Law?

Does the exercise of love in human relations dispense with the Ten Commandments as a guide for ethical and responsible conduct? Quoting this Bible verse: "He who loves his neighbour has satisfied every claim of the law" (Romans 13:8, NEB), some contend that love alone is the norm to follow.

However, the text does not set forth love and law as opposites but as complements. Ostensibly, love is clearly superior to cold law in human relations. On the other hand, without definite moral guidelines, man can in the name of love work himself into many unlovely and unhealthy situations.

What would you think of a neighbor who governed his relationship to you solely by impulses which arose out of the situation involved? Clearly his insistence on exercising situational love apart from law could subject you to tyrannical and brutal experiences.

Would your husband or wife, property, or you yourself be safe from a neighbor who wholly within himself, at any moment, decided what form his love for you should take? Just what would keep this individual from rationalizing adultery, robbery, or even murder in the name of undefined love?

Evidence indicates that the majority of people today have discarded the Biblical concepts of discipline and morality. The rising tide of drug addiction which authorities claim is reaching epidemic proportions and the frequent outbursts of aggression and hostility among all classes of people are but two examples of this trend. According to published reports those under twenty-one years of age commit two thirds of all the crimes of violence (murder, assault, and rape).

Couple with the foregoing the depressing fact that many high school students accept sexual permissiveness as right and proper. They reason that God is dead, the Ten Commandments belong to the dim past, the coming judgment is a figment of the imagination, and the pill is here; so, why not revel in these physical pleasures without regard to consequences?

Of course, the advocates of the new morality and free love tone down the dire results of this so-called liberation from the hang-ups of the past. The Washington *Post* of February 9, 1972, grimly reminds the nation of one of the consequences when it states, "Gonorrhea is second only to the common cold among contagious diseases that strike Americans. Each year it affects more people in this country than scarlet fever, strep throat, mumps, hepatitis, rubella, measles, rheumatic fever, and whooping cough combined, . . . and the disease is totally out of control."

No doubt the most severe consequences of the escalating promiscuity, apart from venereal disease, is the illegitimate pregnancy with its devastating effect on the emotions and personality, consigning youthful idealism and hopes to a premature death.

Who is to blame for this tragic waste of human resources? Who has helped to set in operation the century's greatest social disaster by insisting that abundant love makes discipline unnecessary? Without question, the concept that love and law are totally unrelated has disrupted homes, wrecked college campuses, converted cities into crime jungles, and brought the nation to the verge of chaos.

Who's to blame? The tragic situation does not call for finger pointing, but we should all examine our attitudes and theological leanings in the light of the following statement:

"Those who teach the people to regard lightly the commandments of God sow disobedience to reap disobedience. Let the restraint imposed by the divine law be wholly cast aside, and human laws would soon be disregarded. . . .

"Already the doctrine that men are released from obedience to God's requirements has weakened the force of moral obligation and opened the floodgates of iniquity upon the world" (Ellen G. White, *The Great Controversy,* p. 585).

Rather than leaving the individual wholly to himself to decide what legitimate forms his love for another may take, God, in the Ten Commandments, defines the proper form love should take toward God and man. A man who loves God does not worship other gods, nor bow down before images; he refrains from taking God's name in vain and keeps holy the Sabbath day. These commandments define the first and great love commandment.

Likewise, a man who loves his neighbor, besides honoring his parents, will not kill, steal, lie, or covet anything that is his neighbor's. Thus in all of life's situations the Ten Commandments specifically outline what love demands. Scripture correctly reasons, "Love cannot wrong a neighbour; therefore the whole law is summed up in love" (Romans 13:10, NEB).

If the love spoken of here means anything, it means that such love will never initiate or perpetuate the ugly human behavior forbidden in the Ten Commandments. Obviously, if love annuls law, then such love becomes a meaningless and vapid emotion, totally unrelated to man's best needs and interest, and human existence becomes extremely precarious, if not impossible.

God never intended that law become a substitute for love. In God's plan law keeps man from interpreting love selfishly. Hence true love satisfies "every claim of the law," because the Ten Commandment law has respect to the mutual and loving relationship that should exist between all men.

Rather than depreciating or depriving the law of its sanctions, the love expressed by Christians must be as broad and exacting as the law itself, and the Sermon on the Mount sets forth this nature of both love and law.

As an example, Christ characterizes the lust or hatred residing in the heart as the parent of adultery or murder. In God's sight the desire and the act are synonymous. Social propriety and restrictions may temporarily check the act, but only the love of God motivating human conduct in harmony with the claims of divine law has the power to crucify the unlawful desire.

Christian love and discipline always interlock and cannot be adequately expressed apart from each other, anymore than you can separate the steering mechanism of the automobile from the wheels and expect the car to operate safely and adequately. If automotive, electrical, and atomic power need controls, shall we reason that as highly volatile an emotion as human love shall know no boundaries, checks, and limits? Only in the setting of the Sermon on the Mount can love impel correct behavioral action toward another and expel anything detrimental to the best interest of the object of love.

To be sure, life is complicated and situations arise that defy analysis, but it was so in the days of our Lord. He gave us an example of how to relate to others by accepting God's explicit commandments as a guide and directive in all of life's situations. How else can we understand His words: "If ye keep my commandments, ye shall abide in my love; even as I have kept my Father's commandments, and abide in his love" (John 15:10)?

No matter how perplexing the life situation, Christ never separated an expression of love from God's moral requirements. To all recipients of His love He commanded, "Go, and sin no more" (John 8:11). Doesn't this mean that in order to retain the benefits of His love, the receiver must from henceforth conform his life to clearly expressed moral requirements?

As never before, life today demands action, not irresponsible action that deprives a person of protection against his neighbor's exercise of love without law, but responsible and virtuous action that satisfies "every claim of the law"—the Ten Commandments. Love and law, concern and control, compassion and discipline, these meaningful moral combinations can be realized only in Christ.

"When one surrenders to Christ, the mind is brought under the control of the law; but it is the royal law, which proclaims liberty to every captive. By becoming one with Christ, man is made free. Subjection to the will of Christ means restoration to perfect manhood" (Ellen G. White, *The Ministry of Healing*, p. 131).

The Generation Gap

The plan of moving people into and out of the world poses vexatious problems for young and old. Starting as a helpless infant, each person moves swiftly through youth, eventually slips into old age, and then disappears in a blur of weakness. Some draw the conclusion that arriving ready for action and then marching off in full strength would be much better.

Certainly other forms of biological life assume their full, or nearly full, adult functions at birth. Obviously, no animal's maturing is as long and trying as is man's. In the process, certain complications crop out in a person's relationship with those ahead and those behind, so that each generation seems to be stepping on the other's heel. However, a wisdom greater than man's organized the complex interrelationship, and we would do well to adjust our thinking for the good of all concerned.

Adjusting our thinking does not eliminate the perplexing and, at times, annoying aspects of the generation gap. Listening to some talk would lead you to believe this attitude difference developed in our day, whereas it has always existed. Closing it calls for the exercise of virtues that develop something fine and noble in both generations. Evidently the gap exists for a purpose. Instead of fighting it, why not discover and fulfill its purpose?

Perhaps you know of an experience similar to the following: An academy girl is considering a college career. From the earliest years she and her parents agreed that she should become a medical secretary. Joyfully they examine curricula, colleges, and tuition. Finally they list their preferences and are about to make a decision.

Suddenly the girl announces that she is not going to be a medical secretary but a physical education instructor, and that she is considering another college. Upon recovering from shock, the parents ask, "Why?" She replies that she and her girl friend think that it is best. And how do they know? Well, some other young friend convinced them. Embarked on the collision course, the once quiet family now spends many an evening in heated discussion, tears, stresses, and strains until the problem is resolved.

Or consider the father who owns the best bicycle repair shop in town. It delights him when his son shows an interest in rebuilding old bicycles. One day when the father points out the correct way to adjust the brakes, his son pointedly contradicts him. And where did the son get his superior information? A "guy" from the bicycle factory told him. Stunned, the father wonders what happened to his meek and obliging little lad, so suddenly transformed into an assertive teen-ager.

Ostensibly, unless constantly under the control of God's sweet Spirit, human nature can be harsh to both young and old.

Animals force the young to leave the family den, birds push the nestlings out of the nest, but human beings accomplish the same purpose in a much more difficult manner. Just as a mysterious impulse makes birds migrate at a certain time, so the urge comes causing young people to manifest a restlessness and an impatience with home ties.

In human life this mysterious urge hits about six to eight years before leaving home is feasible, thereby prolonging the period of strain and ambiguity. Just when youth need home the most, frustration and resentment begin to mount. Suddenly everything seems wrong to the children. Parents are unreasonably domineering and awkward. They have embarrassing table manners. Mother wears dated clothes. Father tells flat jokes. Home lacks bright conversation and an intellectual atmosphere. At this time boys start dreaming of far-off lands, and girls wish that they could lower the marriage age a year or two.

The wish to push away from home, drastic though it may seem, is God-implanted. It builds up over a period of years until the youngster has matured enough to make the move. This awkward period calls for patient love, understanding, and the exercise of intelligent self-control by both adults and youth.

Moreover, if the hurts accumulated in the process are not too severe, the mysterious method can work out to a mutually beneficial conclusion. Mark Twain supposedly commented of his father, "When I was sixteen I thought my father was an ignoramus. But when I was twenty-one I was amazed to discover how much progress the old man had made."

Whether we like it or not, the younger generation is born into the governance of the old. There is no other way to come into life. The babe arrives so equipped that he has to be protected, carried, fed, and taught by those who were born earlier. Without parental protection he can never make it.

Seniority, therefore, plays a great role in life. Not without reason, all cultures regard longevity as a distinction which weighs heavily in having the last word. On the average, those who have been learning the longest should know the most, but this the young resent. The implication of their inferiority makes sense, but they just do not like it. That is, until they themselves become adults and parents, and then suddenly the inferiority inference is replaced by a surprisingly knowledgeable sense of assumed responsibility for their offspring.

Why is this?

When answering this question forget the old prejudices and remember some basics. First of all, the same God who implanted the independence impulse in youth also made parents responsible for the care and guidance of their children. As long as they live, parents cannot shake off this sense of obligation. In times of frustration they may wish to transfer it to someone else, but it is always there. Whether the child is ten or fifty, mother always checks his clothes and reminds him to look in both directions when crossing the street. Let a son or daughter leave on a trip and the parents are full of anxiety until the child returns safely. Understandably, this parental desire to protect conflicts with the child's impulse to be independent.

When properly related the two opposing generation impulses can contribute to the tranquillity and harmonious spiritual development of both generations. Obviously it is the Creator's purpose that both young and old should understand their interdependence and then mutually assist each other in closing the gap. When cheerfully implemented, the process develops happiness and security not only in this life but also for the life to come.

That is how it should be and can be, the youth looking to the aged for counsel and wisdom, and the aged looking to the youth for help and compassion. These mutual and endearing bonds of affection will inspire the youth to achieve responsible maturity and comfort the aged as they approach the sunset years.

"Bear ye one another's burdens, and so fulfil the law of Christ" (Galatians 6:2).

Closing the Generation Gap

Parents and children have a mutual responsibility in closing the generation gap. The Scriptures clearly set forth the obligation of the parents to direct wisely and of the children to submit cheerfully in order to become complete persons. Both generations gain when they fulfill their respective roles in the following manner: "Children, it is your Christian duty to obey your parents always, for that is what pleases God. Parents, do not irritate your children, so that they will become discouraged" (Colossians 3:20, 21, TEV).

Why does the human family have to relearn the skills of living every time a new generation appears on the scene? We certainly do not discard the wisdom of the past in the field of art and science. In this respect we benefit greatly from the profundity passed on by our elders.

But the reverse is exactly what happens in the area of human relations. Once weaned, the oncoming crop of babies acts as if wisdom originated with them. It is true that times change and that the intelligence of the ancients needs to be relevantly applied, but the change is a great deal less than most youth think.

When young people mutter, "We are in the 70's; why can't our parents realize that things are different now?" they need to understand that nothing has really changed except the vocabulary and the trimmings. The old mistakes still do not work; the laws of God and nature cannot be amended. Landing on the moon has not changed the law of gravity. In fact, it makes the principle even more important. Neither does modern psychology nor the sexual revolution lessen the sacred obligation to "honour thy father and thy mother."

Coming to the problem of regulating youthful conduct, parents are often accused of assuming an authoritarian and unreasonable attitude. No doubt at times parents do err. On the other hand, do not consider them to be odd and tyrannical freaks for attempting to establish guidelines and rules for the inexperienced family members. Life is disciplinary. Would young people want to live in a family with unconcerned parents? Of course not. So why not accept reasonable regulations as good and necessary?

Anything resembling a step toward marriage likewise arouses intense feelings among young and old. To the parents the friends of a marriageable daughter appear as bright and upstanding young men until one of them begins showing a serious interest. Then by some quirk of parental concern the positive evaluation of the young man fades, and he suddenly looms as a lurking Dracula.

Let's face it. Most parents want their children to marry someone like they married. Do not blame them for this, for in the majority of cases they made a good choice. Candor compels the admission that there are sandbars and submerged rocks in the seemingly placid sea of marriage which could scuttle any matrimonial craft attempting to navigate these waters without prior counsel and direction.

Statistics reveal that marriages which cross religious and cultural lines fizzle out more often than not. Therefore it should not be too surprising when parents express concern. Marriage is a serious venture, and by reason of their experience parents are able to look beyond the exotic to the afteryears when life makes exacting demands on both marriage partners. Therefore youth would do well to listen to someone who has gone over the road before them.

Nowadays numerous books and sermons stress the need of parents' understanding the youth. This is all well and good. But what is wrong with the other side of the coin, youth understanding their parents? Teenagers do go through a restless and unsettling time of life, and they should be handled understandingly. The adult can afford to be sympathetic, for, unless his memory has failed completely, he can remember the time when he was part child and part adult, with the body experiencing mysterious changes. What man does not remember the day when as a boy he awoke to discover that he could no longer sing soprano? Those are trying days for any young lad.

But do you think that it is less trying for adults? They, too, go through difficult times. Suddenly they are neither young nor middle-aged, and everything seems to be wearing out, dropping out, and spreading out. Looking into the mirror each morning they are startled by an aging face looking back at them. Now, as never before, parents need love and consideration from the youngsters.

Truthfully, young people are not mature until they can look at their parents as real people with real problems. If this is necessary on the part of parents in dealing with children, it is equally true for children in dealing with parents.

A mistaken concept is to look upon each other as paragons. The child is the cutest and best mannered in the neighborhood, but one day he becomes a brat. Mother is the most beautiful woman in the world and father is the strongest man; then suddenly everything is wrong with Mom and Dad. Responsible maturity is being able to deal with each other as human beings, neither perfect nor impossible but loved.

Therefore the older generation needs to understand the younger and vice versa. Each can educate the other, but only when he has some understanding of what makes the other one tick. Parents relive through their children. This is neither strange, odd, nor an imposition. It just happens to be the way the human race is organized. When parents want to know where their children have been and what they were doing, it is not because they are inquisitive or critical. They have valid concern because they love their children and obtain tremendous satisfaction in living through them.

Come, now, sit down, and let us reason together. The basic truth is that parents and children were made for each other and consequently need each other's friendship, support, and understanding. Of all people, children, like actors, must have an audience, and parents are the finest. Wholesome and continued positive living is motivated by someone who believes in and hopes for you, who applauds whenever you make any progress. One of the overwhelming sorrows when a parent dies comes in realizing that your best audience and most constructive critic is gone.

What shall we do about it? We have talked and written about the generation gap until we are almost convinced that it cannot be closed. The truth is that it can be.

Home is the place to begin, and the way to begin is by the two generations understanding and bearing each other's burdens. The parents must always care for their children, and there comes a time in life when the children must care for their parents. The most sobering crisis in any life is the discovery that life is about finished. Threescore and ten years may seem a long time to young people, but it is a chilling thought for those who have passed the summit, and life is now all downhill. Youth is not the only time of turbulence.

Who has not witnessed the sad spectacle of neglected and deserted parents? If they will, children can spare parents from this disaster and make their last years a golden sunset. This means giving as much attention to the parents in their declining years as the parents gave to the children in their early years.

Both stages of life have their peculiar problems. God gave both ages their mutual responsibilities. In a Christian home all the members love and care for one another. Therefore, to the younger and to the older generation comes the Word of God: "We then that are strong ought to bear the infirmities of the weak, and not to please ourselves" (Romans 15:1).

Following this counsel goes a long way in closing the gap.

What We Owe Our Youth

Not all youth are callously irresponsible. Many are decent and concerned human beings who are not afraid of challenge and hard work. In addition, they possess some measure of appreciation for sacrifices that parents and former generations have made in their behalf.

On the other hand, the few who burn down buildings, defy lawful authority, wallow in obscenity, and scorn standards of hygiene and morality are most vocal in demanding that society and the church turn the reins of government over to them. In loud, strident tones they deride the horrible world they inherited (as if former generations inherited something better), the hypocrisy of their elders, and the seeming mulish inflexibility of the "establishment."

Without downgrading the valuable role that youth may play in improving the equality of society and the church, let it be understood that simply because youth are bright does not mean that they are always right. High grades, idealism, and a sense of concern do not automatically endow a youngster with a true historical perspective. Some things, such as sound judgment and common sense, are the products of time and experience. Obviously, ranting, protesting, threatening, and the shouting of epithets compare favorably with the tantrums babies fly into when they do not get what they want.

"The youth present their demands"—so runs the usual pattern of life in the world today. In other words the youth seem to be saying, "The world and the church owe us what we are asking for. Now give in or else!"

When the irresponsible and the rebellious shout that the older generation and the church have failed them and consequently owe them something, they are right. We do owe them our love, our patience, and our sympathy, but these virtues have their limits. Discipline and love are not opposites but functions of each other. We are reminded that "the so-called tenderness, the coaxing and the indulgence, used toward youth by parents and guardians is the worst evil which can come upon them. Firmness, decision, positive requirements, are essential in every family" (Ellen G. White, *Testimonies,* Vol. 5, p. 45).

Without question, we have also failed youth by allowing them to get too big for their britches, when a firm hand appropriately applied might have contributed more to their education and enlightenment than any set of modern encyclopedias could ever achieve. "Son," a father reminds his growing son, "just keep in mind that I know much more about being young than you know about being old." So while always demonstrating kindness and understanding toward youth, parents should clearly define well-chosen guidelines, and when the youngster coldly challenges the rules, he should be given a good reason to regret his brashness. Authority should be administered as something not *against* the youth but *for* the youth. Scripture assures, "Correct thy son, and he shall give thee rest; yea, he shall give delight unto thy soul" (Proverbs 29:17).

It may sound paradoxical, but we have cheated our youth by giving them too much. No generation of young people has been so well fed, clothed, and entertained, but no generation so blessed has been so inclined to rebellion and opposition against constituted authority. We have given them everything except a sense of respect and responsibility, and this is evident in their sloppiness of mind, clothes, and manners.

Although it may be too late for some youth to change, it is not too late for others. No one ever gets too old to learn. For the willful and obstinate who insist on disrupting academies, colleges, and institutions of higher learning, we owe a Christlike entreaty and the opportunity to correct their ways. When this procedure fails, we then owe them an escort to the edge of the campus and a one-way ticket home.

Believe me, when that great moment arrives, the loudest applause will come from other young people who want to study, who want to build up the church instead of tearing it down, and who wish to order their lives in harmony with the Biblical doctrines of the church.

To be sure, we owe our younger generation something more than abject surrender to every whim and demand. We owe discipline, leadership, and guidance. We owe our children the kind of teaching that will endow them with respect for worthwhile values and will prepare them when their time comes not only to fulfill their idealism but also to cope with reality.

Furthermore, we owe them an example of how to react to trial, suffering, and disappointment without losing faith in God and the church. Just because things do not turn out exactly as one wishes is no excuse for anyone to disrupt the orderly procedures of a home, school, church, or society.

As parents, teachers, ministers, and church members we owe the youth an example of self-control over our own unruly nature. This is most important, for those who are unable to rule themselves inevitably insist on ruling others. The less control they have over their own selfish impulses, the more they seek to impose their tyrannical drives upon others. A person at war with himself will inevitably war with others. We owe our youth the demonstration of the peace of God ruling in our hearts and in our relationship one with another, regardless of our ethnic and national origin.

"Christ is the only true pattern. . . . God has given them one standard, perfect, noble, elevated. This they must meet, irrespective of the course which others may pursue. But many parents seem to lose reason and judgment in their fondness for their children, and, through these indulged, selfish, mismanaged youth, Satan in turn works effectually to ruin the parents. . . . Children are what their parents make them by their instruction, discipline, and example" (*ibid.*, p. 37).

Finally, we owe our youth the training and development which will help them to give rather than get. Care and concern for others refuses to accept emptiness or apathy. Concern for others is wishing someone well and then turning the wish into practice.

How much one cares is demonstrated not by noise and protest but by the emptying of one's own pocketbook and life. Far too often those who criticize the church and society for not doing more are merely covering up their own refusal to do anything at all. Those most aware of needs within and without the church are usually the ones who work silently and sacrificially to fulfill such needs.

Therefore, let us give our youth what we owe them—a Christian faith, heritage, and character. When everything else fails, this alone will stand them in good stead in the troublous days ahead.

Children Need Association

Sixteen-year-old Betty left home and married a twenty-year-old boy whom both her father and mother considered to be a poor marital risk. The distraught mother wondered why her intelligent daughter would do such a thing without first talking it over with her. She had a right to be dismayed but not surprised. In reviewing the past, she discovered the reasons for her daughter's action.

When Betty was ten years old, Mrs. Brown had taken a full-time job to help pay for some needed wardrobe items. She intended to work for only a few months, but the paycheck had a hypnotizing effect, and she could not bring herself to quit.

Consequently, every afternoon Betty came home from school to an empty house. When Betty's parents did come home, they were too tired to discuss her girlish problems and aspirations. Thus Betty grew up alone, and when she complained about how lonely it was around the house, her mother would shrug her shoulders and say, "You are a big girl now, and you must learn to do things without depending so much on Mother."

That is precisely what Betty did. In her loneliness she invited school friends to her home. Since Mother was not around to assist in the choice of friends, some came whose influence was not the best. Mrs. Brown did not know it, but, while gaining financial security, she lost her daughter. Too late she realized that you cannot neglect young children and later expect them to confide in you.

Wise mothers realize this and live close to their children. At best a mother's time with her children is limited, and every moment must be used to teach them how to differentiate between right and wrong and to implant a sense of responsibility in their young minds. By example and precept a mother must uphold standards of cleanliness, order, and purity.

Furthermore, homelife provides the child with the opportunity to grasp the full meaning of obedience and cooperation. Insignificant as these traits may seem to some, they are tremendously important in our complicated, technological civilization. Life today moves swiftly, often demanding split-second reactions, and those who would survive must understand the meaning of obedience and cooperation. This is true whether one is experimenting in a kitchen or a college laboratory or driving on a freeway.

How well husband and wife cooperate with each other at home, and children with parents, determines the cooperation of youth in classrooms and in group activities. Courtesy, politeness, and regard for others is not taught solely by textbooks but mainly by example.

Someday children will be old enough to consider marriage. In their fathers and mothers they should behold their matrimonial ideals. Over and above the cooking, sewing, laundering, and working for a living, what should youth find in their parents?

Chief among many things, they should recognize their parents as partners in holy wedlock, who are constantly increasing their capacity to care for others and progressing from getting to giving—often giving in to each other. Included in this is willingness to work and pray together, to solve problems through compromises and mutual agreement.

Far too often parents express disagreeable thoughts about each other in the presence of children. They nag or deflate. Unconsciously this engenders hostility in children toward society. Thoughtlessness and selfishness exhibited in the home cannot be shed too easily outside the home.

Especially effective in manufacturing delinquents are parents who periodically turn loose their critical venom upon teachers, ministers, law-enforcement authorities, employers, or neighbors who happen to own a better house or car. This hostile atmosphere spawns youngsters suspicious of and antagonistic to rules and regulations of a well-ordered society.

On the other hand parents can provide opportunities for children to develop inner resources against corrosive pressures of life. Such training is needed more than ever today when correct behavior is effectively undermined by the glowing box in the corner of the living room.

When did you last read the Bible to your children? When did you last take them to an art gallery, or an aquarium, or arrange for them to listen to the music of the masters? Are they acquainted with the wonders of the fields, lakes, and mountains? Unless you supply them with that which is uplifting, they will seek the cheap, the tawdry, and the defiling.

Along with everything else, parents should provide controls for their children. State institutions and penitentiaries are crowded with people who have never learned that controls are a necessary part of life.

Limits to behavior should be established, clearly defined, and firmly enforced. Home is the training school for life in a world of many people. No one can with safety disregard the rules of physics, chemistry, space travel, or sports, let alone the Ten Commandments. It is disastrous to suggest to children that some laws should be obeyed and others disregarded.

The permissive fallacy is that a child can learn good things from bad experiences. In this respect consider the irresponsible counsel of a university professor of psychiatry regarding the problem of alcoholism. In proposing a solution for alcoholism, which, incidentally, has enslaved some eight million people in the country, the eminent educator proposes that children in early grades of school be given group instruction in social drinking.

Amazingly the learned professor suggests that children should begin with very weak drinks, such as sherry and a little water, and that the amount of alcohol should be gradually increased through the high school and college years. Drinking small amounts slowly with other persons would, the professor believes, facilitate social relations, relaxation, and a feeling of well-being. "Alcohol is here to stay," the professor continues, "and people must learn to develop a healthy attitude toward it."

Let us develop this reasoning a bit further. Lying is here to stay, but small children should not be taught how to prevaricate properly in order to promote satisfactory social relationships. Stealing, cheating, profanity, narcotics, dope, marijuana, are with us, but should little tots be given lessons in these vices?

The professor is wrong—dead wrong! Children and youth should be taught to abstain from anything evil and not merely to be temperate in its use. Such an education can be obtained best within the confines of a well-regulated Christian home. As Solomon wisely said centuries ago, "Train up a child in the way he should go: and when he is old, he will not depart from it" (Proverbs 22:6).

A Murderous Swallow

"Wine gives false courage; hard liquor leads to brawls; what fools men are to let it master them, making them reel drunkenly down the street" (Proverbs 20:1, TLB).

Americans swallowed approximately 300 million gallons of liquor in 1971. This dubious pleasure cost them about seven billion dollars. Nine million alcoholics, nearly 10 percent of the nation's working force, paid a far greater cost. These unfortunate individuals constitute the prime factors in the absenteeism and inefficiency presently plaguing business and industry and the ensuing annual loss to the nation's economy of about 15 billion dollars. The big swallow hurts financially.

All this may seem rather impersonal and distant. However, this machine age demands split-second reactions, and drinking is no longer a private matter.

It becomes everybody's business because the use of alcoholic beverages by nine million chronic drinkers and sixty million social drinkers poses a murderous threat to anyone who noses his car into a street or highway. Authorities claim that of the 50,000 highway fatalities in 1971, drunken drivers caused 28,000 deaths, besides being responsible for multiplied injuries. The big gulp also has murderous implications.

An equivalent death toll at sea would require the sinking of seven to ten giant ocean liners with all hands aboard. In the air it would mean 250 jet-plane crashes—about twenty a month or five every week. One can well imagine the uproar and protests that would sweep the country if large planes started dropping from the skies at the rate of five a week.

Because it does not happen just that way, we are tempted to sit with hands folded while an entrenched industry spends 250 million dollars annually to advertise a product which produces a comparable carnage in a less spectacular way. In addition some sincere but naïve individuals readily accept the liquor industry's contention that liquor revenue goes a long way in defraying the cost of state and federal government.

The obvious mollifier in the foregoing claim is that liquor taxes lighten the citizens' tax burden. On the contrary, the disturbing facts show that for each dollar of liquor revenue collected, the taxpayer pays out an additional eleven dollars to offset the baneful results of the liquor traffic.

Obviously something has happened to our personal and national values when we spend more money for alcoholic beverages than for education. Surely, judging by the amount of money laid out for each, many value liquor more than bread and milk. The nation spends nearly five times as much for intoxicants as for all religious and private welfare agencies combined. An aroused social conscience should demand a rethinking of these values and a stark recognition of what alcoholism is doing to our individual and collective moral influence.

What can we do?

To begin with, everyone agrees that no one desires the condition of alcoholism. But many ignore the fact that this sordid state results from a "moderate" use of alcohol. The ultimate degradation can never be separated from the occasional drink.

Who is the moderate drinker? He is that drinker who believes that alcohol provides him with some positive social values—relaxation, conviviality, distinction, and a release from life's irritations. Here you have the psychological breeding ground where confused, frustrated, lonely, and frightened people rationalize their need for drinking.

The liquor industry capitalizes on the personal need for identity, success, and acceptance. Have you ever seen a liquor advertisement picture a drinking man or woman in a disheveled or silly appearance? Instead you see poised and masterful men; beautifully gowned and well-behaved women. No thick-tongued speech. No drowsy and slit-eyed appearance. No murders. No slums. No divorces. No bankruptcies. Sad to say, such public institutions as magazines, newspapers, radio, and television participate in the deception when they feature such befuddling allurements as a means and method of social success.

For this reason, if for no other, a torrent of indignation mail should pour into state and federal legislatures protesting laws which permit the sale of liquor in grocery stores, drugstores, department stores, gasoline stations, and so on. And why spare the so-called public servants (newspapers, magazines, radio, television) who sell their birthrights by splattering liquor advertisements over newsprint and airwaves while editorially deploring the drunken highway slaughter and urging citizens to drive cautiously?

Reprehensible as it is for citizens to drive while intoxicated, it is equally bad for trusted public servants to urge citizens to purchase and imbibe a benumbing product which impairs judgment and doubles or triples the reaction time needed for braking a car. This serious flouting of delegated social responsibility should be stopped.

Youth, businessmen, ministers, and women (women are devastatingly effective in this arena) should mobilize and attack through PTA organizations, service clubs, ministerial associations, press, radio, and television. They should aim to strip liquor of its glamour and reveal it as the cause of divorces, financial waste, crime, injuries, and traffic deaths.

While condemning the liquor industry, we need to deal kindly and compassionately with the victims of the nation's major narcotic drug. Having been tricked into dependence upon alcohol for needed relaxation and conviviality, they need to see it as a dangerous substitute for the ability to relax and converse as moral individuals. They should see in the use of strong drink to forget problems and shortcomings an obviously futile escape attempt. In dealing with the problem we shall have to use understanding more than criticism, and assistance more than condemnation.

Experience teaches that the road back from alcoholic degradation to complete healing begins with the love of God and the grace of Christ. Alcoholism can become a past chapter in one's history when he believes and acts upon the following spiritual fact: "He that hath the Son hath life; and he that hath not the Son of God hath not life" (1 John 5:12).

Why the Spirit?

The French painter Emile Renouf in his painting "The Helping Hand" depicts an old fisherman seated in a boat with a little girl beside him, perhaps his granddaughter, both their hands on a huge oar.

He looks down at her fondly and admiringly. Apparently he has told her that she may assist him in rowing the boat. In her desire to help, she feels as though she is doing a great share of the task. However, his strong, muscular arm actually propels the boat through the waves.

Likewise God grants us the privilege of sharing in the development of our personal Christian characters and the advancement of His work in the earth. However, we must ever keep in mind that we cannot perform either task in our own strength but only as God works in and through us. While He directs us to put our hands upon the oar, we must ever be aware of the source of our power.

What is that power? "And I will pray the Father, and he will give you another Counselor, to be with you forever, even the Spirit of truth, whom the world cannot receive, because it neither sees him nor knows him; you know him, for he dwells with you, and will be in you" (John 14:16, 17, RSV).

The Scriptures give prominence to the Holy Spirit as the unique power of Christianity. Other religions have their founders, sacred books, and laws, but they lack the Biblical doctrine of the Holy Spirit.

Only by the Holy Spirit can an individual achieve personal communion with God. Those seeking access to the Father must know the Son, and to know the Son one must be directed by the Spirit. The apostle Paul summed up this comprehensive truth when he said, "For through him [Christ] we both have access by one Spirit unto the Father" (Ephesians 2:18).

No matter how penetrating or persuasive, truth without the Holy Spirit merely produces certainty of knowledge but not of salvation. Ideas, ethics, and philosophical definitions save no one. Paul discovered this in ancient Athens, and we would do well to recognize it today.

God does not conceal Himself from men, but men, by their own course of action and puffed-up conceits, distort their understanding of the Almighty. Like the Jews of Christ's day, far too many people today seek a God who is relevant to their times and practices. To be acceptable God must conform to their standards. In the name of relevance men insist that God serve one human system or another. If He does not, men presume Him irrelevant or even dead.

But God continues to be God, and He will not be stampeded into actions alien to His character merely to accommodate the dulled and sinful hearts of men. God continues to be God even when men shun the only means whereby they may understand Him.

In just what manner does the Spirit reveal God to men? Through the Holy Scriptures, since only in this written form could the continuity and accuracy of God's thought be guaranteed through the centuries. Man can have confidence in this revelation, "for the prophecy came not in old time by the will of man: but holy men of God spake as they were moved by the Holy Ghost" (2 Peter 1:21).

Truth is mighty, and it prevails; yet it is only mighty and prevailing when there is life behind it. Man certainly needs truth today but he also needs perception to see and power to follow that truth.

Therein lies the close and essential connection between the Word of God and the Spirit of God. The one provides the truth; the other the power. The one bestows the light; the other the life. This makes the Biblical revelation personal in source and destination; personal because it is the revelation of a Person to a person, of God to man. When accepted and acted upon this manifestation of God effects a transformation in the life of the individual who accepts it as such.

Why do men question God's ability and power to take a drab and useless life and transform it for time and eternity? If the forces of nature can take the elements in a handful of sand deep in the earth and transform them into a beautiful, fiery opal, or those in clay into a lovely amethyst, or black carbon into a glorious diamond, shall nature's God be limited in what He can do with and for men?

Let it always be kept in mind that God sees men not as they are but as they might be when controlled and molded by His divine Spirit. No man has sunk so low, or has been so far removed from God by sin, that he is beyond the miracle-working and saving power of God. If that man wills, he can, by the love of God shed abroad in his heart by the Holy Spirit, achieve the dignity of true manhood and sainthood in this world.

Contrasted by the sordid works of the flesh which mark a man's life before conversion, the fruit of the Spirit stands in bold relief, for it is "love, joy, peace, patience, kindness, goodness, faithfulness, gentleness, self-control" (Galatians 5:22, 23, RSV).Here is the acid test of conversion and the Spirit's possession of the life, for "you will know them by their fruits" (Matthew 7:20, RSV). All other professions are vain.

Regarding the latent possibilities wrapped up in forgotten kernels, the late Professor Huxley stated that the soil of England contains tropical seeds in a bewildering variety. Brought by birds and winds, these tropical potencies lie buried. Huxley states that if England could have tropical heat for twelve months, the nation would be amazed by the luxuriant blooming of strange plants throughout the entire countryside.

We never fully sense the potential that lies buried

in our own lives and in the lives of men and women around us, a potential placed there by God and awaiting the warming influence of heaven. In our chilled lives the gospel seeds lie dormant. Consider the changes that would take place in the church and in the world if the church would begin praying and seeking for the heat of heaven, the Holy Spirit.

The chill in today's spiritual atmosphere increases with religious apostasy. A group of so-called Christian theologians, claiming to pioneer a new understanding of God, have virtually dismissed the Holy Spirit from their thinking. As a result, a plethora of human speculation now colors and controls their concept of God. To the degree that these religious teachers deny dependence upon the Word and the Spirit for an understanding of God, to that degree do they compound confusion as to man's origin, redemption, and foreordained future.

This attempted ascendancy of human reason over the revealed Word of God simply revives the ancient heresy that man can achieve his destiny without God. Why depend upon God to get to heaven, they reason today, when you can get to the moon and to Mars in a spaceship?

Their muddled theology also envisions the New Testament as the product of overwrought and overenthusiastic apostolic imaginations and thereby totally irrelevant to modern thought, at least without sophisticated explanations. Disillusioned by the skepticism permeating the pulpit, the man on the street slowly succumbs to the ensuing secularism and in practice adopts the pagan maxim—"Eat, drink, and be merry, for tomorrow we die."

Without question, the remnant of God face a blasé, cynical, and scoffing generation. What, then, are we to do? Shall we stand still, wring our hands, and bemoan the evil? Or shall we address ourselves to the task and in the power of God take the gospel everywhere?

As in the past, before the church breaks through to the world, the Spirit must break through into the lives of church members. Call it the "latter rain" or anything else, it simply means the control of God, through the Holy Spirit, of our very lives, homes, schools, and churches.

All will agree that such an outpouring of God's Spirit must be preceded by individual heart-searching and forsaking of sin. Cost what it may, this soul cleansing needs to be sought by all who profess to be God's people. When experienced, such consecration expresses itself in brotherly love and unity, and then it spreads outside of the church in a zealous concern for lost men and women everywhere.

As God lives, the everlasting gospel will break through to modern man and compel his attention before the end comes. The driving power attending the message and messengers will be that of the Holy Spirit working through dedicated men, women, and youth.

Christ Is That Power

While you sit in your living room quietly reading, possibly sipping a hot drink, the earth zooms through space at 1,100 miles a minute. Nothing around you betrays this fantastic speed. There is no swaying, jarring, or stomach-raising centrifugal pull as the earth banks at terrific speed in its 595-million-mile orbit around the sun.

Simultaneously our sun, pulling its flock of spinning planets, orbits within the vast Milky Way Galaxy with blinding speed. Throughout the journey this massive and flaming orb continuously emits enough energy to melt a 3,000-foot layer of ice surrounding it in ninety seconds. Surprisingly, in the process of supplying light and heat, the sun loses four million tons of hydrogen per second; yet it has never suffered a power shortage.

Far beyond the sun is the great star Betelgeuse. Compared with the sun's diameter of 864,400 miles, that of Betelgeuse is 350 million miles. Farther out beyond the Milky Way billions of blazing suns, glittering and swirling galaxies, sweep in orderly procession around the center of the universe—the throne of God.

The mind reels and staggers as it tries to fathom the far-flung and intricate, yet smooth, operation of the universe. Who set it going? What power maintains it?

As if anticipating our questions, the prophet Isaiah answers, "Lift up your eyes on high, and behold who hath created these things, that bringeth out their host by number: he calleth them all by names by the greatness of his might, for that he is strong in power; not one faileth. . . . Hast thou not known? hast thou not heard, that the everlasting God, the Lord, the Creator of the ends of the earth, fainteth not, neither is weary? there is no searching of his understanding. He giveth power to the faint; and to them that have no might he increaseth strength. Even the youths shall faint and be weary, and the young men shall utterly fall: but they that wait upon the Lord shall renew their strength; they shall mount up with wings as eagles; they shall run, and not be weary; and they shall walk, and not faint" (Isaiah 40:26-31).

Understandably, the wisdom that created the suns and the planets, and which sustains their awesome orbit in the widest expanse of space, may well beget in us a sense of reverential awe. But greater wonder, the same Creator descended to reach down to a sin-infected speck of dust called earth and there planted His cross. And from that cross there now flows an inexhaustible stream of redeeming grace and sustaining power to all who believe.

The universe originated in the mind of God. As the

active agent in Creation, Christ spoke it into existence. The laws governing the universe merely express the mind, will, and purpose of the Creator. He, and not some aptly phrased mechanistic law, holds the universe together. Documenting this truth Paul states, "He made the world, . . . upholding all things by the word of his power" (Hebrews 1:2, 3).

Likewise the plan of salvation originated in the heart of God. As the active agent in redemption Christ voluntarily carried out the plan of His Father. "For God so loved the world, that he gave his only begotten Son, that whosoever believeth in him should not perish, but have everlasting life" (John 3:16).

Even as the physical sun lightens the world, so does the Son of God lighten every man that comes into the world. Every noble thought, every holy desire, every pure ideal, and every good deed has its source in the divine Son of God. The call today is for every man to open his heart and receive Christ as Saviour and Lord. The power of God is unto salvation.

We would do well to remember that the power to redeem is no less than the power to create. In either case, Christ is that power and that power is Christ. Besides creating and upholding the cosmos, Christ makes available His justifying, sanctifying, and glorifying power to those on earth who submit themselves wholly to Him. He excluded no one; whosoever will may receive the power of Heaven.

God grants the power, not to satisfy the demands of pride, doubt, and unbelief, but to magnify His name and to exalt Christ. Living Christ's life, overcoming inherited and cultivated tendencies to evil, obeying God's commandments—this is incontrovertible evidence of man's possession of a power outside himself.

Therefore no one, no matter how weak, need fail. Trusting completely in Christ means trusting One who keeps the stars on course and who alone "is able to keep you from falling, and to present you faultless before the presence of his glory with exceeding joy" (Jude 24).

The Title to the Kingdom

"Not every one that saith unto me, Lord, Lord, shall enter into the kingdom of heaven; but he that doeth the will of my Father which is in heaven" (Matthew 7:21).

All men will admit a desire to gain heaven. But their desire and the requirements for heavenly citizenship do not match. Since the requirements run counter to some cherished habit or custom, men have endeavored to establish their own terms of entrance.

They often buttress their terms with strained Biblical interpretations. Some rest in the claim that their church has the "keys" to the kingdom and can admit or shut out whom it will. They feel that as long as they belong to the right church, their chance to make the grade is good, character notwithstanding. Others place much emphasis upon one aspect of God's character —love. Still others platitudinously declare that the practice of the "golden rule" will achieve heaven, regardless of what else one may or may not believe about God. These, and many other conceptions of what constitutes a title to heaven, place much force upon profession which requires practically no change in life-style, and very little, if any, emphasis upon obedience and discipline which necessitate self-denial and sometimes even inconvenience.

It takes no special wisdom to see that this one-sided emphasis disqualifies men for earthly kingdoms, let alone heavenly. Even a liberal and optimistic thinker like Harry Emerson Fosdick years ago found it necessary to comment: "When I searched volume after volume of modern addresses and sermons, I did not run upon any that dealt with respect for and obedience to authority. There were plenty on freedom, on the emancipation of the individual, on the outgrowing of old restraints, but few, if any, upon the necessity and glory of being mastered by what rightfully masters us. The impression began to sink in that our orgy of lawlessness is not an accident or merely a postwar psychological reaction, but that it is the natural fruitage of deep-rooted tendencies in our thinking which have affected alike our religion and our law."

To remedy the situation, to retain national integrity and honesty, to make communities and cities safe places for decent people to dwell in, the religious leaders of the land need to revise their sermon notes to include a greater emphasis on obedience to law as the foundation stone of personal and national character. No sane and rational individual, irrespective of religious belief, will deny the need of this emphasis and practice if we wish to retain any semblance of law and order in our day.

The Necessity of Law

Strange, twisted human reasoning maintains the necessity of obedience to civil law for earthly survival, but at the same time dogmatically denies the need of obedience to God's law. Such reasoning would make men more particular about their earthly affairs than God is about His heavenly affairs. To the contrary, revelation and nature, God's two lesson books, clearly define Him as a God of law and order. Notable is the statement found in Psalm 103:19, 20: "The Lord hath prepared his throne in the heavens; and his kingdom ruleth over all. Bless the Lord, ye his angels, that excel in strength, that do his commandments, hearkening unto the voice of his word."

The phrase "ruleth over all" implies a well-ordered and a law-abiding universe. Obviously, this explains the reason why Lucifer and his followers were expelled from heaven, for "God spared not the angels that sinned, but cast them down." With sin being defined as "the transgression of the law," and since Lucifer sinned from the beginning, it is unmistakably clear that the foundation of God's kingdom from the beginning of time rested on law (2 Peter 2:4; 1 John 3:4, 8).

Likewise, nature testifies to the reign of law. Above us the myriads of suns, constellations, planets, and satellites rush through space in perfect harmony and obedience to law. On the earth below we find the vegetable and animal kingdom operating within well-defined bounds of law. Plant potatoes and you harvest potatoes, not roses. A duckling is no sooner hatched than it waddles off to the pond and "takes to water like a duck." Let a chick try the same thing and it will drown.

Men have discovered that heat, light, energy, electricity, chemistry, and mathematics operate within precise boundaries of law. This fact makes calculation and civilization possible. We have taken nature's laws into account in the architect's office, in the machine shop, on the farm, and even in the kitchen. We have discovered, many times to our sorrow, that these laws must be obeyed, and that slighting them courts disaster. We know that whenever a boiler explodes, or a dam bursts, or a roof caves in, or a bridge collapses, or even when the homemade bread does not taste right, someone, somewhere, somehow, has transgressed a law.

While fixed laws which cannot be disregarded govern everything in nature, man alone is amenable to moral law. Like the laws of our physical world, the moral law exists whether man recognizes it or not. Man may scoff at the law of gravitation, but the scoffing will not soften the fall when he steps off a roof. Similarly, man may disregard the prohibitions against stealing, murder, lying, lust, coveting, profanity, but his calloused indifference does not protect him against the inevitable penalties of pain, loss of liberty, suffering, and finally death.

Men of every race and clime bear witness to the moral law of God, the Ten Commandments, as found in Exodus 20:3-17. Even those who have never read the written law find their consciences testifying to it. "For when the Gentiles, which have not the law, do by nature the things contained in the law, these, having not the law, are a law unto themselves: which shew the work of the law written in their hearts, their conscience also bearing witness, and their thoughts the mean while accusing or else excusing one another" (Romans 2:14, 15).

The universality of the following laws are recognized by all as constituting the standard of right and wrong.

The first commandment forbids the worship of anything created, and requires worship of the Creator only (Exodus 20:3).

The second forbids the worship of images or the works of men's hands as an act of homage to God (verses 4-6).

The third requires all to revere and honor God's name and forbids profanity (verse 7).

The fourth defines the use of time. Six days are to be used for labor, but the seventh day is God's holy Sabbath, reserved for rest and worship (verses 8-11).

The fifth reveals the duty of children to parents (verse 12).

The sixth protects the lives of all (verse 13).

The seventh preserves the virtue of the family (verse 14).

The eighth protects the property of all (verse 15).

The ninth prohibits lying (verse 16).

The tenth forbids coveting anything that belongs to others (verse 17).

In essence, the Ten Commandments define the specific relationship of man to God and of man to man. At the first reading, the commandments may appear as a law of mere prohibitions. There is a reason for this, however. God recognized the evil inclinations that reside in every human heart: "The heart is deceitful above all things, and desperately wicked: who can know it?" (Jeremiah 17:9). He pointedly opposes their gratification. In this way, through the claims of moral law, God makes Himself intelligible by crossing man's path just where he feels inclined most to wander. Thus the commandment is not only a fence for man's protection; it is also a positive demand for obedience.

The Nature of the Law

"The law of the Lord is perfect" (Psalm 19:7). "The law is spiritual." "The law is holy, . . . and just, and good" (Romans 7:14, 12). The law of God is not holy, perfect, just, and good merely because it is a law. Since law presupposes a personality and cannot exist apart from personality, the Ten Commandments are all this because they are an expression of God's nature.

God is perfect, spiritual, holy, just, and good, and the law is not a thing *made*, but coexistent with God. The law is eternal because God is eternal. As long as God exists, His law will exist. The two are eternally bound up with each other. To abolish one you must abolish the other. "From everlasting to everlasting, thou art God." "All his commandments are sure. They stand fast for ever and ever, and are done in truth and uprightness" (Psalms 90:2; 111:7, 8).

There is a very real reason why God reveals His nature and character to men in the form of a moral requirement. All Christians pray, "Thy kingdom come," but few take the trouble to investigate the nature of the coming kingdom. The apostle Peter states that we "look for new heavens and a new earth, wherein dwelleth righteousness" (2 Peter 3:13).

The new kingdom will be peopled with an obedient race of men and women because they took seriously the task of preparing for the kingdom of God. They will be those who took time to find out what God required as a preparation for heavenly citizenship, and then they persevered in that preparation.

In this they followed the unerring example of their Saviour, who promised, "If ye keep my commandments, ye shall abide in my love; even as I have kept my Father's commandments, and abide in his love" (John 15:10).

Like a golden thread in an exquisite tapestry, so will God's law throughout eternity be interwoven with His nature, His government, His kingdom, and His people.

The Law Cannot Be Abrogated

Even as the truest compass or chronometer may be turned out of its way by magnetic variations and thus become untrustworthy, so the truest conscience may be turned out of its way by the passions, vices, and lusts of life. When the chronometer gets out of adjustment, it can be adjusted with the perfect timekeeper—the sun. When one's conscience becomes confused in this world of evil, the only way to adjust it correctly is to test it by the great moral timekeeper of the universe—God's Ten Commandments. Here alone is the safe definition of right and wrong. "I had not known sin, but by the law." "By the law is the knowledge of sin" (Romans 7:7; 3:20).

Unthinkingly, some religionists often state that the love of God and the death of Christ have made obedience to the Ten Commandments unnecessary. They point to their stern requirements as being out of harmony with the spirit of the New Testament. They further argue that the Ten Commandments belong to the old covenant, and point out the impossibility of keeping them, since everybody breaks them. From this polemic they go on to discourse vaguely about the "comments of Christ" replacing the law of God. Such reasoning would have one believe that the pardoned sinner has the right to continue flaunting the law which he violated. As if in direct answer to this reasoning, Paul declares: "Do we then make void the law through faith? God forbid: yea, we establish the law." "What shall we say then? Shall we continue in sin, that grace may abound? God forbid. How shall we, that are dead to sin, live any longer therein?" (Romans 3:31; 6:1, 2). Twice Paul uses the strongest language possible to refute the reasoning that pardon and love make obedience to God's law unnecessary.

Who suffers when a man sins, the law or the sinner? Every man born into this world tries to play with the laws of God. In time some grow wiser and obey, while others continue in their disobedience and suffer the consequences. Adam first disobeyed and billions of men have followed in his steps; yet God's laws remain intact. "All his commandments are sure. They stand fast for ever and ever" (Psalm 111:7, 8).

But the lawbreakers—you will find their fragments throughout all history. The ruins of Egypt, Babylon, Pompeii, Jerusalem, and Rome tell eloquently the tragic story that "the way of transgressors is hard" (Proverbs 13:15). Should one wish more recent exhibits, let him visit the prisons, the reform schools, the skid rows, and the cemeteries. Here one will find an unanswerable argument concerning the immutability and unchangeableness of God's law. The Scripture states that "sin *is* the transgression of the law" and that "the wages of sin *is* death." The word *is* indicates that both sin and death are with us today, and our prisons and cemeteries confirm the fact. Since these penalties of the law are present, then the law also is present.

The word *whosoever* in 1 John 3:4 ("*whosoever* committeth sin transgresseth also the law: for sin is the transgression of the law") removes sin, law, and death from a confinement to any one age, dispensation, nation, or people. Since sin and death are universal in their binding claims, it stands to reason that the law is likewise. Sin and death prove that no moral being can escape from God and from the penalty of disbedience to His unchanging law. "Now we know that what things soever the law saith, it saith to them who are under the law: that every *mouth* may be stopped, and *all the world* may become guilty before God" "for *all* have sinned, and come short of the glory of God" (Romans 3:19, 23).

The fact of the sternness of the commandments of God in no way proves them out of harmony with the spirit of the New Testament. Those who would point to the Sermon on the Mount for precepts which replace the Ten Commandments point us to precepts which condemn far more severely than do the Ten Commandments. The Giver of the Ten Commandments on Mount Sinai and the Preacher of the Sermon on the Mount are one and the same—Jesus Christ.

The Sermon on the Mount is the republication of the Ten Commandments in a more spiritual and penetrating form. Going beyond the overt acts, these precepts teach us that the angry word is murder and the lustful look is adultery. Far from finding any release from obedience to God's law, one finds in these teachings of Christ only greater condemnation. "Whosoever [again that all-inclusive word] therefore shall break one of these least commandments, and shall teach men so, he shall be called the least in the kingdom of heaven" (Matthew 5:19).

Finally, the death of Christ upon the cross settles beyond all controversy the impossibility of abrogating

God's law. Could the law have been abolished, and sin been disposed of in this way, then Christ would not have needed to come and die for our sins. Since God's law is the revelation of His inmost being and could not be done away with without doing away with God Himself, Christ willingly came to satisfy the demands of the law, lest the world perish. "Christ Jesus . . . became obedient unto death, even the death of a cross" "that he by the grace of God should taste death for every man" (Philippians 2:5-8; Hebrews 2:9).

God could not do away with His moral requirements simply because man chose to disobey, or lessen the requirement because sin lessened man's ability to comply. To have done so would mean that God either did away with or lessened His own holiness and righteousness. While God did not change His law by one hair's breadth to save a world of sinners, He did do something else—"God so loved the world, that he gave his only begotten Son, that whosoever believeth in him should not perish, but have everlasting life" (John 3:16).

The law reveals God as unchanging in His demands for holiness, righteousness, and obedience to His subjects, but the cross of Christ reveals the great lengths to which God went to make possible that holiness, righteousness, and obedience in His subjects without abrogating the law.

The Necessity of Grace

Whereas the law reveals holiness and righteousness, it reveals such only in its mandatory aspects. In other words, the law has no power to justify men and subsequently make them obedient, holy, and righteous. That is what Paul meant when he said, "By the deeds of the law there shall no flesh be justified in his sight" (Romans 3:20).

Someone and something apart from the law must enter into man's disabled life and enable him to obey and thus impart holiness and righteousness. That something is the love of God, and the grace of our Lord Jesus Christ brought to man through the office and person of the Saviour. "But God commendeth his love toward us, in that, while we were yet sinners, Christ died for us," "for by grace are ye saved through faith; and that not of yourselves: it is the gift of God" (Romans 5:8, Ephesians 2:8).

Conclusively, then, obedience is not the cause of salvation, but the result of salvation. A saved man is an obedient man. Christ saves His people *from* their sins, not *in* their sins. "He that hath my commandments, and keepeth them, he it is that loveth me" (John 14:21).

But how can the love and grace of God effectually make one obedient who has been accustomed to disobedience? Only by such a man's beholding and understanding the great sacrifice that God made in his behalf when Christ died on the cross. Meditating upon the love of God eventually dispels a man's hostility toward God and changes his attitude toward God's requirements. "Herein is love, not that we loved God, but that he loved us, and sent his Son to be the propitiation for our sins." "Hereby perceive we the love of God, because he laid down his life for us" (1 John 4:10; 3:16).

That the love of God is as much a part of God's nature as are His holiness and righteousness is the good news of salvation. It is as universal and applicable as His law and as available as the air we breathe. God provides it for sinners like you and me. Love pleads, "Come now, and let us reason together, saith the Lord: though your sins be as scarlet, they shall be as white as snow; though they be red like crimson, they shall be as wool." "If we confess our sins, he is faithful and just to forgive us our sins, and to cleanse us from all unrighteousness" (Isaiah 1:18; 1 John 1:9).

Love and grace save us not by ignoring obedience and holiness but by vicariously satisfying their demands. Furthermore, by changing our attitude toward God, they also create a desire in our hearts to obey His commandments. Infinitely more than that, the love of

God supplies the power for obedience. "For this is the love of God, that we keep his commandments: and his commandments are not grievous" (1 John 5:3). What was once a burden, the love of God changes into a delight; and that which we once shunned, we now love. All this is accomplished by the love and grace of God in Christ.

Many years ago a young lad left mother and home to seek a career at sea. While wandering over the face of the earth he neglected to write his lonely mother. The pleasures and interests of life were so absorbing that they ruled out any time for the one who loved him most. Years passed, when suddenly memory of mother and home came upon him like a flood. He recalled his boyhood days and his mother's love. Tears misted his eyes as he thought of her untiring vigil at his sickbed, the days she spent in making, cleaning, and mending his clothes, and her willingness to go without in order that he might have the necessities of life. With heavy heart he recalled her pleading for him to remain at home and her final embrace and words of endearment as he walked out of the house into the world. Memory having done its work, the lad, now a grown man, decided to return to home and mother.

On his way home his conscience plagued him. "Is Mother alive? Does she still love me? Am I worthy of her love? Will she receive me after these many years away from home?" These doubts constrained him to write a letter telling her of his decision to return home, asking her forgiveness, and requesting that she hang a white sheet on the clothesline in the backyard as evidence that he was forgiven and would be accepted home again. He further stated that if this white sheet was not in evidence on a certain day, he would regard it as a sign that she no longer cared for him to return home, as his prolonged absence had destroyed her love for him.

Approaching his home cautiously on the specified morning, the wayward but now repentant son looked for the sign of forgiveness and acceptance. He looked, and then rubbed his eyes in amazement. Not only one sheet, but the entire clothesline was covered with sheets, and from every available window additional sheets were fluttering the signals of a loving mother: "Come home, Son, come home; Mother still loves you."

My friend, likewise you may have wandered far away from God and His requirements. You have walked and lived in opposition to the God who loves you. Now your heart is made tender as you think of Him who loved you and gave Himself for you. You wish to return to God, but doubts plague you. "Does God still love me in spite of my sins? Will He forgive me? Will He accept me?" I can understand your questions. You want evidence to dispel the doubts holding you back.

Look at Calvary. See there the greatest evidence that God loves you and will forgive and accept you. See there the One hanging between heaven and earth on a cross. He hangs there broken, because the law could not be altered. He hangs there for your sins and mine. "This is a faithful saying, and worthy of all acceptation, that Christ Jesus came into the world to save sinners; of whom I am chief" (1 Timothy 1:15).

Friend, where will you spend eternity? To every man in his sober moments there comes the question of eternal destiny. The Bible clearly teaches of a hereafter for those who accept the salvation offered by the Son of God. Christ clearly stated the title to the coming kingdom: "Not every one that saith unto me, Lord, Lord, shall enter into the kingdom of heaven; but he that doeth the will of my Father which is in heaven" (Matthew 7:21).

All others will be denied entrance, regardless of their profession. The following text makes that unmistakably clear: "Know ye not that the unrighteous shall not inherit the kingdom of God? Be not deceived: neither fornicators, nor idolaters, nor adulterers, nor effeminate, nor abusers of themselves with mankind, nor thieves, nor covetous, nor drunkards, nor revilers, nor extortioners, shall inherit the kingdom of God. And such were some of you: but ye are washed, but ye are sanctified, but ye are justified in the name of the Lord Jesus, and by the Spirit of our God" (1 Corinthians 6:9-11).

Your heavenly Father wills that you become obedient, holy, and righteous. But you cannot become this apart from the love and grace of Christ.

If you have never accepted Christ before, why not now? If you have backslidden from God, why not return now? If you have become careless and indifferent concerning sacred duties, such as prayer and Bible study, why not start again now? If you have not been the kind of father, mother, son, or daughter that you should be, why not start now? Why not accept now all that God has supplied for you in Christ?

Tomorrow may be everlastingly too late!